Cover photo by Benh LIEU SONG / Wikimedia

Written by: Stacey Kuyf

Edited by: Bruno Luis

Contents

Introduction to Turkey

There are few destinations which offer the history, architecture and culture found in Turkey. Because it straddles the continents of both Asia and Europe, Turkey has long been a strategically important location, hosting some of the biggest figures in history, including Julius Caesar and St Paul.

One of the biggest draws to Turkey is the food, and sociable Turks use eating as a way to catch up with friends and family. Be sure to try the baklava, along with plenty of olive oil lathered vegetables, and spicy dishes from throughout the country.

Of course Istanbul is a must-visit, with more than 2500 years of history, traditions, culture, and landmarks but it's far from all this country has to offer.

Turkey's charm can be found throughout the country. Here you'll find ancient bazaars, magnificent ruins, sandy beaches, and majestic mountains. The sheer diversity between the eastern mountains and Aegean beaches has to be seen to be believed, and while foreigners can easily find themselves in nightclubs and markets, Turkey offers plenty of chances to explore the less-visited eastern quarters.

Romans, medieval Armenians, Byzantine Christians, Lycians, and Ottoman sultans have all had a part in making Turkey what it is today, and the caves of Cappadocia, ruins of Ephesus, and infinity pools of Pamukkale will astound and impress even the most seasoned traveller.

#1 Istanbul

© Flickr / Moyan Brenn

The sheer history of Istanbul can be almost overwhelming, and this mix of Asian and European culture has hugely impacted the food scene. Be sure to try the authentic Ottoman food, the meat and fish typical of Turkish food, and one of the popular Turkish desserts. Famous for its vibrant nightlife, the city offers many bars and nightclubs for party animals.

Those who like to shop will also have plenty to do, as the modern shopping centres, combined with the Grand Bazaar and excellent local designers, offer some of the best shopping you'll find anywhere. With palaces, mosques, bazaars, and towers, Istanbul boasts both incredible architecture and breathtaking views.

Istanbul is likely to have been inhabited by people around 3000BC, but the history of Istanbul generally begins around the 7th century BC, with Greek colonists establishing the colony of Byzantium after King Byzas consulted an oracle of Delphi. The decision was sound, as Istanbul's location has shaped its history.

In the 300's the city became a party of the Roman Empire, and Constantine the Great rebuilt the entire city, with the aim of making it unique, giving the city monuments similar to those found in Rome. In 330, Constantine announced that the city was the capital of the Roman Empire, subsequently renaming it Constantinople. Constantinople enjoyed years of prosperity, however after emperor Theodosius I died in 395, his sons divided the empire. Constantinople became distinctly Greek as part of the Byzantine Empire, and greatly grew in wealth, becoming the centre of commerce, diplomacy, and culture.

The city's success drew attacks for centuries as it became a prime target for those who saw it ripe for conquering. Constantinople became the centre of the Catholic Latin Empire in 1204, before it became bankrupt, and was eventually conquered by the Ottomans in 1453. The city was renamed Istanbul, and was ruled by the Ottoman Empire until their defeat by the allies during World War I. Today you'll find many of Istanbul's historical areas on the UNESCO World Heritage list, and with a population of more than 14 million, the city continues to grow and thrive. Istanbul's architecture paints a picture of its unique history, with century old buildings standing next to modern skyscrapers. Mosques, synagogues and churches represent the religious background of those who live in the capital and manage to coexist peacefully. Landmarks to visit include, Topkapi Palace, Hagia Sophia, the Grand Bazaar, the Blue Mosque, Basilica Cistern, Galata Tower, and the Süleymaniye Mosque.

© Wikimedia / Dmgultekin

The Grand Bazaar

The best way to explore Istanbul is on foot, enjoying the smells of rich spices, the sounds of many different languages, and the ever-constant call to prayer. A Bosphorus Cruise is an excellent way to see an overview of the city and explore both the Asian and European shores of the waterway, with mansions and century old palaces on display. The Archaeology Museum also offers some of the richest collections of classical antiquities in the world, so spend a day soaking up the immense history in the city, and be sure to wear appropriate clothing when visiting mosques.

#2 Cappadocia

© Flickr /Mr Hicks46

Cappadocia is 750kms from Istanbul in the Anatolian region of Turkey, and features a remarkably barren landscape which some have called Martian or lunar-like. This is the place which inspired the backdrop of Star Wars, and nature has carved out rock pedestals which man then used to build underground cities and cave homes.

The weird rock formations are a sight to see, and the region is also famous for its excellent artisans which include rug makers, pottery craftsmen, and winemakers. Cappadocia is home to one of the most amazing landscapes in the world, with soaring rock formations and deep valleys dotted with chapels, tombs, temples, and homes.

The Persians, Alexander the Great, the Ottoman Empire, the Hittites, and the Byzantine Empire have all governed the region, which has more than 200 tunnel towns and underground villages spread over one hundred square miles.

Neolithic tools and pottery point to an early human presence in Cappadocia, with remains dating from approximately the 3rd millennium BC. The beginnings of the chambers and tunnels are still unknown, with some archaeologists believing they were started by the Hittites in 1200 BC, and others believing that they must have been made before metal, as the tunnels were hewn using stone.

Cappadocia was a religious refuge by the fourth century as Christians fled the persecution of Rome and established communities in the area. Byzantine monks excavated many of the dwellings and monasteries, each beautifully decorated and painted, and are still well-preserved today.

The attractions and activities in Cappadocia centre around the unique landscape, and of course the caves. Visitors can stay in a cave suite and enjoy the history of the place, as well as all of the comforts of home, including gourmet breakfasts, jacuzzi-fitted bathrooms, and electric heating. One of the best ways to see the area is from a hot air balloon. Take a sunrise ride, and you'll get an idea of just how incredible the rock formations are. Bring a camera, as seeing the hundreds of hot air balloons with brightly colored canopies combined with the barren landscape is truly a bucket-list experience.

The Town of Göreme

Derinkuyu is the deepest underground city, extending to a depth of approximately 60m and able to hold just under 20,000 people. It is a truly fascinating place, but it is best to hire a guide as you won't find any signage.

At the centre of Cappadocia is the town of Goreme. It is favorite touring base for many travelers due to its many hotels and inns, and its proximity to many of Cappadocia's top attractions, including the remarkable Goreme Open-Air Museum.

#3 Ephesus

© Wikimedia / Benh LIEU SONG

Cleopatra, Mark Anthony, and St Paul have all visited the city of Ephesus, which peaked in the 2nd century, when almost 300,000 people lived there. The city became one of the main economic and cultural centres of the ancient world before declining after the 7th century.

The ruins are impressive, and include a gymnasium, baths, a theatre, and the Library of Celsus; however Ephesus was famous for its temple to Artemis, which was one of the seven wonders of the ancient world.

While the city was inhabited as the Bronze Age ended, it has been ruled by various cultures, including the Greeks, Persians, and Romans. Liberated by Alexander the Great during 334BC, Ephesus became Roman in 133 BC, and was made capital of Asia Minor during 27 BC by Augustus. Immigrants and merchants were attracted to the city, and the population quickly grew.

St Paul lived in the city for three years during the AD 50s, and many Christians believe that Mary, the mother of Jesus, settled here with St John, who wrote his gospel in Ephesus. Ephesus was at its peak during the 1st and 2nd century, however the harbor continued to silt up despite numerous rebuilding efforts. Eventually the harbor was lost, marking the decline of Ephesus.

There's a reason why Ephesus is one of the major sightseeing attractions in Turkey. The glorious monuments provide plenty of opportunities for photos, and the well-preserved theatre, huge library, and the Temple of Hadrian shouldn't be missed.

The Ephesus Museum displays some of the best finds from the city, including an exquisite statue of Artemis, along with the Gladiator Room which has some of the best pieces from the excavation of the gladiator cemetery.

While only one column remains of the original Temple of Artemis, this was once one of the Seven Wonders of the Ancient World. The site was originally occupied by a huge stone platform where an image of the goddess presided, and rooms were located underneath where offerings were made.

Theatre of Ephesus

Meryemana, another major tourist attraction located 8km from Ephesus, is where many say the Virgin Mary died. A shrine dedicated to the Virgin Mary was discovered in the 19th century by a French Priest after a German nun had visions of the site.

The site is open to the public but expect to be rubbing shoulders with plenty of other tourists. It is best try to explore Ephesus and Meryemana early in the morning when they are less crowded.

#4 Marmaris

Located in an exceptional location in southwest Turkey, along the Turkish Riviera, Marmaris is both a tourist resort and a port town. While the population was 30,957 in 2010, 1.65 million tourists visited Marmaris and the surrounding districts during 2014. Marmaris has a charming old town, a spiffy marina, and a historic castle, along with plenty of bars, clubs, and restaurants.

The name Marmaris comes from the Turkish word 'Mermer', which means marble. This is because the rich deposits of marble in the region, and the significant role of the town's port in the marble trade.

While no one knows exactly when Marmaris was founded, the town was previously called Physkos. The Carians settled in the area on their way from Crete, with the town becoming part of the Carian Empire during the 6th century BC. They used the natural harbor as a military base, but it also enhanced rade between the Aegean Islands and Rhodes.

King Attalo surrendered Physkos to Rome in 138 BC, and the city was ruled by Roman generals. Physkos then joined the Ottoman Empire in 1425, with Kanuni Sultan Suleyman changing its name to Marmaris.

He oversaw the building of the famous castle of Marmaris, however some historians believe that there was already a castle in Marmaris from 3000BC, and King Attalo simply rebuilt the previous castle. Renovation has been continuing at the castle since 1979, and it is now a museum with seven galleries.

Marmaris is now a huge resort city, with hotels suiting all types of budget, hundreds of cafes, restaurants, and bars; and visitors can spend time swimming in the city centre, or take a boat trip out to some of the other coves.

The area is also popular with scuba divers, and taking a Turkish bath is the perfect way to relax after a long day of diving. For those who are wondering, you can leave your swimsuit on, since men and women congregate in the same room.

Marmaris Centre

The Marmaris Grand Bazaar has hundreds of outlets, stalls, restaurants, and shops, and the covered walkways protect visitors from the heat. Marmaris Castle is a must-visit, where you can wander the exhibition hall, galleries, and courtyard, while learning about the history of Marmaris.

The castle also offers excellent panoramic views of the city, and you may spot some tortoises lounging in the grass.

#5 Antalya

Once described as "the most beautiful city on earth" by Ataturk, Antalya is a vibrant and interesting city on the Turkish Riviera. Head just north of the city and you'll find Karain, which has remnants of the oldest settlement ever found in Turkey.

Today the city is a modern metropolis with an old-fashioned, small-town feel. Visitors can jump on one of the many buses which travel between beaches, most of which offer water sports such as waterskiing and surfing, and all are good spots for kids and families.

Antalya was founded by Attalus II in the second century BC, who immediately named the city Attaleai. Since then it has been continuously inhabited, with the Romans following Attalus, (Emperor Hadrian visited in Ad 130) before the town became part of the Byzantine empire.

In 1207 the Turks snatched the city from the Byzantines, followed by the Ottomans in 1391. The Ottoman rule meant relative stability for 500 years, but after WW1 the Ottoman Empire had been divided up by the Allies, and Italy grabbed Antalya in 1918.

The newly independent Turkey recaptured the city in the War of Independence in 1923, and from the 1970s the town has transformed from a tiny town into one of the largest metropolitan areas in Turkey - largely due to tourism.

The city has attracted a large range of travellers, including Paul the Apostle and Ibn Battuta. It now has a multicultural community of Jews, Christians, and Muslims, with millions of visitors each year.

For those interested in history, Antalya is a treasure trove, with plenty of historical sites waiting to be explored. The Antalya museum is excellent, and features enormous sarcophagi, well-preserved Roman statues, and even a jawbone which belonged to St Nicholas, also known as Santa Claus. Hadrian's Gate, which was erected in the name of Emperor Hadrian in Ad 130, is now part of the town wall and well worth a visit if you're interested in Roman history.

Hadrian's Gate

The ancient city of Termessos sits 30 km north west of Antalya and is a protected archaeological site within Güllük Dağı National Park. There is much to see in Termessos including a bath complex and gymnasium, and the incredibly well-preserved Greek style theatre set on the edge of a gorge.

Another option is to head 11 miles east to Perge, which lies on a massive area of ruins, and features a Roman theatre, and columns from when the apostle Paul visited.

#6 Oludeniz

© Wikimedia / Dan Taylor

Oludeniz is home to a sheltered lagoon, next to a national park, with a long sandy beach and Mt Baba watching over the sea. Essentially, it's a tourists dream come true.

With its natural beauty and excellent location contributing to its status as one of the most visited destinations in Turkey. You'll find Oludeniz in the Fethiye district in southwestern Turkey, and the beach is one of the most photographed in the world

The town itself doesn't have much in the way of history. The narrow entrance to its harbor meant that it wasn't favored as a port settlement in ancient times, therefore it was mostly used as a quiet fishing hamlet.

The area surrounding the town is where visitors will find most of the interesting history. In ancient times south-western Turkey was known as Lycia, and boasts a heritage stretching back more than 3000 years. In more modern times, the city has been close to flash points in the ongoing territorial rivalry between Greece and Turkey.

Oludeniz emerged as a popular tourist destination after it was first developed during the 1960s, with the Turkish government declaring the area surrounding the lagoon as a national park.

Active visitors may want to hike part of the Lycian Way, which is a 500km trail running all the way to Olympus, and considered to be one of the top ten epic walks in the world.

The town is also world-famous for its paragliding, and its unique panoramic views make it one of the best places in the world to try the sport. Snorkelling and scuba diving are popular water activities here, and local diving agencies provide certification courses.

Try to avoid peak season if possible, as May to October sees a huge influx of tourists and British citizens who own holiday homes in the town.

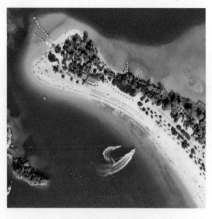

Ölüdeniz Beach

While the town itself may not have many historical sites, visitors won't need to travel very far to find some. Above Oludeniz you'll find a ghost town called Kayakoy in the mountains, which has been deserted since 1923.

The population swap meant that all of the Greeks who used to live here were forced to move back to Greece. The town is well worth a visit since the streets have been left empty by fearful Turks wondering if the Greeks cursed the town.

#7 Bodrum

Each summer more than a million tourists flock to the beaches, clubs, and boutique hotels in Bodrum. Unlike many of the other Turkish getaways, it has an elegance and serenity that makes it stand out. Bodrum has only recently gained popularity, and older residents can still remember when it was a small fishing village.

Ironically, the town used to be where those who didn't agree with the new Turkish republic were punished by being sent into exile.

Herodotus, who is widely known as the father of history, was born in Bodrum (although it was then known as Halicarnassus) in 484 BC. He believed that Bodrum was founded in the 12th century BC by the Dorians, who were followed by the Carians.

The region came under Persian rule in 546, with the city reaching its peak around 353BC when it was famous for its sailing, trade, and boat building, and became the capital of the Satrapy of Caria.

King Mausolus ruled Caria from here, and after he died, Caria was ruled by Artemisa II, who was both his sister and wife. Artemisa built a huge Mausoleum and grand tomb in honor of her brother and husband, which became one of the seven wonders of the ancient world, before it was destroyed in the 14th century by an earthquake.

Between 1415 and 1437, the Knights of Rhodes built Bodrum Castle in honour of St Peter. The marble and stones from the destroyed Mausoleum were used to construct the castle. The castle was then used as a prison after 1895, but was then converted into a museum in 1962.

Bodrum is fascinating, and is both a historical site, and a playground for tourists. It was a fishing village up until the 1960s, but is now full of clubs, bars, restaurants, scuba diving companies, and hotels. The city is perfectly located on the western coast of Turkey, and only 20 minutes to the Greek Island off Kos.

A favorite pastime for many tourists is heading down to the harbor in the morning, finding a small, independently run boat for a day trip, and taking a relaxing sail through the Aegean. A tour of Bodrum Castle is a must, as it has been fully renovated and houses the Museum of Underwater Archaeology.

Bodrum Castle

This is a town perfect for wandering, with cobbled back-streets, small restaurants serving delicious Turkish food, and the weekly farmers market presents a good chance to talk to the locals and browse the tourist trinkets.

#8 Side

This once tiny fishing village now sees a constant stream of visitors from around the world, and with plenty of Hellenistic and Roman ruins scattered between shops, it makes it easy to imagine how the town looked thousands of years ago. Side is located on a small peninsula, and combines chic shops, late night bars, and boutique hotels with the ruins of an ancient city. With an untouched old town flanked by gorgeous, sandy beaches, it's easy to see why the town has been consistently gaining in popularity since Cleopatra and Anthony used to visit.

Side's history dates back to the 6th century BC. Located in the Anatolia region, Side was one of the earliest settlements in the area. Its name means pomegranate, and it's believed that Side was settled around the 7th century BC before coming under the rule of everyone from the Lydians to the Turks.

During the 5th century BC, Side showed its richness and strength by minting its own coins. Alexander the Great took the city in the 4th century BC without a fight, and it was a relatively peaceful period for the region. In 190BC the town allied with Antiochus III who was king of Syria and fought against the Rhodian fleet, but the city was occupied after they lost the naval battle.

During the 1st century BC, Side became a slave market and was occupied by pirates. When the Romans arrived the pirates departed, and the Romans brought a new period of prosperity to the city. Side began a steady decline from the 4th century on, with earthquakes and frequent raids contributing to its decline. Eventually Arab raids destroyed the city in the 7th century AD. It had prosperity on and off through the next few centuries before being abandoned around the 12th century. Now Side once again flourishes as one of the top tourist destinations in the country.

The ruins in Side are among the most impressive in Asia Minor, and include well-preserved city walls, a large theatre complex, the public bath which was restored as a museum, and the square agora. The ruins also include an aqueduct, three temples, and a nymphaeum which is a natural water supply. Spend a day exploring the ruins, and be sure to head to the Temple of Apollo during sunset, as it is an excellent time to take pictures at the 2,000 year old temple.

© Flickr / W. Lloyd MacKenzie

Temple of Apollo

The town has a beach on each side, both with jet-skis and banana boats entertaining tourists, and beach bars and sun loungers to relax on dry land. East beach is more windswept, less crowded, and sees more locals, while you'll find more families at the sheltered West Beach as it's closer to the hotels and has calmer waters.

Side presents an amazing opportunity to have both a historical and fun vacation. With a nightclub smack bang in the middle of the ruins, and restaurants looking out at historical sites, visitors leave feeling like they've had the best of both worlds.

#9 Ankara

The capital of Turkey, Ankara is also the second largest city in the country (after Istanbul). The city is a huge student town, along with being the centre of the government. Sure, you won't find many Ottoman palaces here, but the youthful, vivacious atmosphere, booming restaurant scene, side walk cafes, and dynamic street-life mean that anyone traveling to Turkey should take the time to visit.

Located on a rocky hill, and in one of the driest places in the country, Ankara is still one of the greenest, with a large amount of green spaces for residents and visitors to take advantage of. Formerly known as Angora, the history of the region goes all the way back to the Bronze Age Hattic civilisation. Under the Phrygians the city grew in size and around 1000BC the city benefited from huge expansion following a vast migration of people from Gordion.

Like most regions in Turkey, the city changed hands throughout the centuries. It was controlled by the Phrygians in the 10th century BC, followed by the Lydians and Persians. In the 3rd Century BC the Galatians took Ankara, naming it Ancyra which means "anchor", and making it their capital city.

The city then fell to the Romans, the Byzantines, and finally under the leadership of Ataturk it was made the capital of the Turkish Republic after the National War of Independence.

Ankara is inexplicably a little-known city, even though it's larger than most cities in the United States and United Kingdom, and many visitors to Turkey assume that Istanbul is the capital of Turkey. While you may not see the stunning landscapes found elsewhere in the country, there is still plenty to do in the capital city.

Visit Anitkabir, which is the Mausoleum of Mustafa Kemal Ataturk. The size and grandeur is impressive, and it's an excellent way to learn more about the history of the region.

Kizilay is a trendy area where you'll find outdoor markets, designer retail shops, stylish restaurants, and chic cafes. This is the "downtown" area of the city, and where most of the "cool kids" hang out. It's also where most of Ankara's important memorials and monuments are found, which include Guven Park, Republic Square and the Grand National Assembly of Turkey.

© Wikimedia / Bernard Gagnon

Anitkabir

While the historical Old Quarters may be fairly touristy, (still far less than those in Istanbul), they're still well worth checking out, especially if you're in the mood for bargaining.

#10 Pamukkale

© Wikimedia / Antoine Taveneaux

Pamukkale, known as "Cotton Castle", is famous for not only its unique geological formations, but also the lesser-known historical remains. The town gets its nickname from the waters which are full of calcium-oxide, and flow down the slope of Caldag, located north of the ruins. This has caused the deposits to build up on the plateau over thousands of years, forming travertines and hot springs.

People have been bathing in these pools for thousands of years, so be sure to bring a bathing suit. But also spare a few days to visit the ruins surrounding the pools as well.

Originally named Hierapolis, it appears that the city was founded by the King of Pergamon-Eumenes II. In 133BC it became subject to Rome, and in 17BC it suffered from a huge earthquake which completely destroyed the city.

Hierapolis is mentioned in the Bible, and ancient tradition suggests that Philip died in Hierapolis, possibly around 80AD. Unfortunately it's not quite clear which Phillip is meant, as it could be either Philip the Apostle, or Philip the Evangelist.

Excavation and restoration work has been going on since 1957 at the site, which has been a health spa since it was under Roman rule. The hot springs are still believed to have healing properties, and many people travelled to the site over the centuries in order to cure their various sicknesses. Today, the city is a World Heritage Site and a hugely popular tourist destination.

Obviously the travertine terraces must be visited, and while visitors can no longer walk on the terraces, you can still try out the natural spa. If you need to relax, this is the place to do it, so book a treatment in one of the natural pools, which flow at a rate of approximately 400 litres per second.

The Sacred Pool offers visitors the unique opportunity to actually swim amongst antiquities. Columned porticoes once surrounded the pool during the Roman period, before earthquakes knocked them into the pool.

The Pamukkale Museum is worth a visit, it has attractive displays in both English and Turkish, collections of sarcophagi, jewellery, coins, and many architectural fragments, as well as amazing statues and reliefs.

© Wikimedia / Brocken Inaglory

Limestone Wall

The theatre of Hierapolis has been well preserved, and the stage buildings are decorated with gorgeous reliefs. The North Necropolis (graveyard) is home to more than 1200 tombs, including house-shaped tombs, sarcophagi, and tumuli, some with Jewish inscriptions.

#11 Kusadasi

© Flickr / Joe Pitha

Kusadasi is the busiest cruise port in Turkey, and while it doesn't have the size of Marmaris or the sights of Bodrum, the discos, Irish pubs, and sea views give it a memorable atmosphere. While its name technically means "Bird Island", the town is most well-known for the views of turquoise water and the ancient city of Ephesus in close proximity. Unlike many Turkish towns it remains relatively down to earth, regardless of the many passengers from the hundreds of cruise ships docking for a day or two.

It's believed that the earliest settlements were by the Carians and Lelegians around 3000BC. The mild climate allowed residents to grow grapes, figs, and olives on the fertile lands surrounding the city. Around 564 BC Kusadasi was invaded by the Persians, in 200BC it was dominated by the Romans, and then with the fall of the Roman Empire it became a state of the Byzantine Empire. Huge earthquakes almost completely destroyed Ephesus, and the Byzantines were forced to abandon Kusadasi to find a new port and road for trading.

Over the centuries Kusadasi was settled by Greek, Jewish, and Armenian merchants, and later came into control of Venetian and Genoese sailors and traders who established consulates here.

In 1413 Kusadasi was ruled by the Ottoman Empire as it was in an advantageous position at the end of the Silk Road. During the Ottoman reign, many new structures were built, some of which can still be seen today. Kusadasi was invaded by the Greeks after the First World War, and in 1922 it finally became part of the Turkish republic after a long struggle. Today it's an excellent jumping off point to visit historical points of interest in the area, and is a rejuvenating environment for a holiday.

Near the waterfront you'll find the "downtown area" which is quite modern and has an open air bazaar, along with many other stalls. While the hawkers can be a little annoying, visitors can still find some good deals as long as you practice your bargaining.

Those who love the outdoors will want to spend some time in Dilek National Park, which is government protected and covers thousands of hectares. Here you'll find ideal trekking and photo opportunities, along with bird watching and the chance to see wild boar roaming throughout the paths.

© Flickr / Kusadasi-Guy

Ladies Beach

For something a little different, head to the Aqua Fantasy waterpark, which even has an adjoining hotel if you can't tear the kids away.

You can also book a boat tour to learn more about the area, cruise the coastline, and visit small bays and coves. Or if you simply want a day of relaxation you can sunbathe and swim at one of the many beaches, Ladies Beach being one of the popular ones.

#12 Konya

© Wikimedia / Akkoyun

Konya is one of the most ancient settlements of Anatolia, and is important among both Christians and Muslims. While Konya is an economic powerhouse and a busy university city, it's also very conservative and you'll find a maze-like market and ancient mosques rubbing up against the more contemporary part of Konya around Alaaddin Tepesi- a large student hang out.

Konya is located right next to the Silk Road, and just three hours from Ankara. It's known as the city of Whirling Dervishes, and you'll find plenty to see and do in the area.

The history of Konya goes all the way back to prehistoric times, and it's believed by researchers that a settlement was established here in approximately 6000-5000 BC, making it one of the oldest urban centres on earth.

St Barnabas and St Paul both visited the city on their journeys through Asia Minor around 50AD, and while St Paul chose to preach in Konya, they angered both Gentiles and Jews and were forced to leave the city.

During ancient times the city was called "Iconium", and the Phrygians established a settlement there after the Hittite empire collapsed. From the 7th to 9th century the city was subject to Arab incursions and was taken from the Byzantines by the Seljuq Turks in 1072, before being renamed Konya.

Konya was the capital of the Seljuk Sultanate of Rum from around 1150 to 1300, and this was a time of great prosperity, when many architectural marvels were built in the area.

Inexplicably, few Westerners make the journey to Konya, which is a shame since this important religious centre is crammed full of monuments and museums demonstrating Seljuk splendor.

Those who stop by will usually just visit the Mevlana Museum along with the tomb of Mevlana Rumi, but the city has much more to offer, especially for those interested in Turkey's history.

The Museum of Wooden and Stone Carving is a good place to see wooden and stone sculptures, along with animal reliefs. Alaeddin Tepe is fun for people watching, and the locals come every evening to talk and sip tea in the gardens. You'll also find the excavation site of the palace of Alaeddin Kaykobad here, which was built according to Arabic design and features a wooden ceiling, large pillars, and 42 antique columns.

© Flickr / Kyle Taylor

The Whirling Dervishes

While the archaeology museum may not be much to look at at first glance (it does need a face-lift), the collection is excellent and gives quite the "treasure hunt" atmosphere.

#13 Izmir

While you may not have heard of Izmir, this liberal city is a centre of commerce and a good base if you're planning to do some travel through the west of the country. Its laid-back feel and its Jewish, Armenian, Greek, and Levantine heritage make Izmir quite different from the rest of the country. The city is also developing quite a reputation for its civic and cultural foresight, and its International Arts Festival is a must-see if you visit in June or July.

Izmir's history stretches all the way back to around 3000 BC when the city was founded by the Trojans. Homer was born here, and is thought to have lived in the city around the 8th century BC. Izmir was invaded, destroyed, and rebuilt several times, until Alexander the Great began constructing a castle at the top of Mt Pagos around 330BC. The Pergamons took the city in 290BC, before ceding to the

Romans in approximately the 1st century BC.

The Romans managed to keep the city before the Selcuks grabbed it in 1076AD. By now Izmir was an important port, and a cosmopolitan city, so this began a turbulent time for the region. From 1098 to 1426 the city passed between the Byzantines, Selcuks, Crusaders, Turks, and finally the Ottomans who held it until the 2nd world war when the Greeks invaded.

Finally Izmir was taken back by the Turks during the National War of Independence in 1922, and remains both commercially important and cosmopolitan, with some of the more reserved Turkish regarding the city with a deep degree of suspicion.

Take a walk along the Kordon, which is a coastal path circling most of the centre part of the city. It also acts as a central hub for families and friends, and is bursting with trendy restaurants and bars with outstanding views of the bay.

The Arkas Museum is small, so if you don't have much time it's good place to visit to get a feel for the history of Izmir without losing most of your day. If you're a wine drinker, the Yedi Bilgeler Winery is a hidden gem and also has excellent food available for lunch, and beautiful grounds to walk around.

© Flickr / Filip Maljković

Izmir Clock Tower

The Izmir Clock Tower is located in the main square. The historic Clock Tower is a symbol of the city and a great place for photo opportunities.

The Old Bazaar is more manageable than the one in Istanbul, and has plenty of little spots to take some downtime with a coffee.

#14 Fethiye

© Flickr / Kemal Cenk Sarioglu

Located on the south western coast of Turkey, Fethiye may be a tourist town, but it's popular for a reason. The town is a great place to relax and unwind on the beach, and the perfect base for those who would like to tour inland Turkey.

Fethiye used to be known as Telmessos, and was one of the most important cities of the ancient Lycian civilisation. While there isn't much information known about the founding of the city, most historians agree that Fethiye dates back to around the 5th century BC.

According to Lycian legend, the name Telmessos originates as the god Apollo, who fell in love with Agenor, a beautiful girl and the youngest daughter of the Phoenix King. He disguises himself as a dog to gain the love of the shy princess, and after he reappears as a man their son Telmessos was born, with his name translating as "land of lights".

In 547 BC, Telmessos was captured by Harpagos, a Persian general, and the city joined the Persian Empire. Alexander the Great appeared in Telmessos in 334-333 BC, and the city subsequently surrendered to him. The city then passed between the Romans, Lycians, Ottomans, and finally the Turks. In 1934 it got its present name, Fethiye, in honour of Fethi Bey, one of the first Turkish combat pilots, who died tragically on a mission.

The city was levelled by an earthquake in 1958, which luckily spared the remains of the ancient city of Telmessos. Half a century later, it's once again one of the most prosperous cities of the western Mediterranean, and surprisingly low-key and laid back for its booming growth.

Fethiye's natural harbor is one of the finest in the region, and the surrounding countryside is packed with interesting historical and scenic sites waiting to be explored.

Paragliding is especially popular in Fethiye, and most people take off from Babadag Mountain for some of the best paragliding views in the world. Taking a boat trip or chartering a yacht is also very popular, as there are plenty of picturesque islands around the bay.

If you feel like taking a stroll, head to Paspatur, which is the Old Town in Fethiye. There are many different Turkish and International restaurants, along with shops, spice stands, and cafes.

© Flickr / Jorge Franganillo

Markets in Fethiye

The Cadianda Roman Ruins in Uzumlu are just 20 minutes from Fethiye, and have managed to keep all of the natural character and charm of a traditional Turkish village. Once in Cadianda there are over 3 kilometres of ruins to explore and excellent views over Fethiye.

#15 Alanya

Alanya is a resort city in the Antalya Province in southern Turkey. Its strategic position meant that it was a stronghold for many empires over the years, and its natural attractions, Mediterranean climate, and historic heritage have made it a popular place for tourism.

A few decades ago Alanya was a sparsely populated town, but a recent economic boom means the downtown area can now often remind one of Las Vegas.

However there are plenty of hidden charms in the region, including a Seljuk castle, impressive fortress complex, ruins, and local restaurants.

While there may not be much known about the early history of Alanya, it's evident that the city was crucial to many an empire over the centuries. The city is thought to have been founded by the Greeks and for a time was quiet and peaceful, until Cilician pirates used the town as a base so they could terrorise the coast. Eventually the Romans arrived, destroying the pirate fleet in 67BC.

After the fall of the Roman Empire the city came under Byzantine influence. The Byzantine city then fell to Alaeddin Keykubad in 1221 who named it Alanya and decided it would be his summer residence. After WW1, the city was given to Italy, before being returned to the Turkish republic in 1923. The population exchanges and war were particularly harsh in the region, but now Alanya is back on the up.

Alanya is breathtakingly beautiful, and an ideal place to visit for those who like to combine relaxation with the chance to visit some historically important sites. The new town has been developed, and feels more touristy than anywhere else. So if you want a sense of historic Alanya visit the old town, which boasts huge city walls and ancient stone streets, along with lovely views of the surrounding scenery and nature.

It may be surprising, but bowling has become increasingly popular here, and it's a good way to meet some locals and have some fun. Those who like to dive will love the scuba diving along the Mediterranean coast, and the environment in Alanya makes it ideal, with the climate allowing all forms of diving throughout the year, including deep-sea diving for experienced divers.

Alanya Castle

Cleopatra Beach is a good beach for swimming and tanning, and there are also some excellent historical sites to visit, including Alanya castle, the remains of Seljuk village, the Damlatas Caves, and the Red Tower. The Archaeology and Ethnography Museum is also a great place to visit to learn more about the area.

#16 Dalyan

© Flickr / audi_insperation

Located between the popular districts of Fethiye and Marmaris in South-west Turkey, Daylan could easily be another huge, bustling resort, but instead is a natural paradise with some of the most unique attractions in Turkey.

Daylan is set inland and is a former trading seaport next to the Dalyan river. While it's certainly popular with tourists, the city is still a peaceful holiday spot, and boasts picturesque landscapes, along with hot springs and mud baths for those who need some pampering.

While Daylan and the surrounding area is missing the historical timeline found in Istanbul, the impressive Lycian tombs are a step back in history. Although tourists can't access the tombs, the city also sits next to the incredible ruins of Kaunos which are accessible to the public.

Daylan was once a trading seaport, and there is evidence of residency in the area since the 10th century BC. Daylan was abandoned during the 15th century AD, and excavations from 1966 revealed Byzantine city walls, an acropolis, Roman baths, a basilica, and a 5000 seat theatre.

The city narrowly escaped the perils of bad urban planning during the 1980's when a proposed tourism development was going to be built on Iztuzu Beach, which is a breeding ground for endangered sea turtles. After many celebrities championed the cause, the beach was declared a protected area in 1988, and is now known as Turtle Beach.

Visitors can choose from a large range of shops, hotels, restaurants and bars, and can buy souvenirs at the weekly market. There are also daily excursions which will take you to the many attractions nearby, or hiring a car can be a good way to discover the hidden gems of the area.

Kaunos is well worth a visit, it is an ancient city which was once an important seaport, but is now 8km from the coast. The city walls are from the 4th century BC, and there are six temples to explore, along with the Acropolis and rock tombs.

© Wikimedia / Maria Jonker

Iztuzu Beach

The mud baths are a must, and both locals and tourists travel here to sit in the warm sulphur pool.

Iztuzu Beach (or Turtle Beach) is where you can see turtles nesting from May through to October, and the turtle sanctuary is located at the end of the beach, where you'll find sick and hurt turtles being nursed back to health in huge tanks.

#17 Mardin

Mardin is one of those unmissable spots, and if you're traveling to Turkey it's a good place to wander through bustling markets and gawk at old buildings. While you'll be rubbing shoulders with plenty of other visitors during summer, now is the time to go since the Turkish government is upping their efforts to get more tourists visiting this historic city.

Mardin was called "Marde" by the Persions, "Maridin by the Arabs, "Marida by the Byzantine, and even "Merde-Mero-Merdi" when it was in the hands of the Syriacs. Once it was occupied by the Turks it was finally named Mardin.

It would be simpler to ask who hasn't invaded here, as the city has been conquered by everyone from the Assyrians to the Ottomans. The history alone makes Mardin the perfect stop for those traveling through southeastern Turkey.

Excavations in the area around Mardin show that it has been settled since around 4500 or 3500 BC. The city was home to Assyrian Christians during the 5th century, and they were followed by the Arabs who occupied Mardin sometime between the years of 640 and 1104.

The Ottomans took the city in 1517, and in the early 20th century most of the Assyrian Christians were forced out. Approximately 600 Christians remain in the city, which is still using 11 churches, albeit on a rotational basis. In 1923 Mardin joined the Republic of Turkey, and was made the administrative capital of the province.

Deyrulzafaran Monastery is one of the oldest monasteries in the world and is one of the gems of Mardin. Although the monastery is still in use, tours are available for visitors. Another highlight of Mardin is the gorgeous old theological college (Zinciriye Medrese). It was founded in 1385, and remains one of the best-preserved buildings in the area. The complex includes a mausoleum, two inner-courtyards, and a domed mosque with amazing panoramic views up on the rooftop.

While the collection at the Mardin Museum is small, it does contain some beautiful artefacts, including Bronze Age and Assyrian pottery. The restoration of this 19th century stone villa is impressive, and wandering through the rooms is a good way to imagine how the local merchants would have lived so long ago.

Deyrulzafaran Monastery

Mardin Castle looms above town, so bring some good walking shoes for the steep path leading up to the fortress.

The castle dates from the Roman era, and was extended during the 15th century so residents could seek refuge if the town came under attack.

#18 Kas

© Flickr / Fredi Bach

While you won't find the best beaches in the Mediterranean in Kas, it does make an ideal base if you want to explore the surrounding area. Adventure junkies will be in their element here, as it's a hub for scuba diving, hiking and kayaking, with some great wreck diving just off shore.

The town was once a fishing village (like many of these coastal towns in Turkey), and is still relatively unspoilt, although a large chunk of its revenue comes from tourism. Despite the many new hotels, Kas has still retained its charm, and the waterfront cafes, small beaches, and mix of ancient and modern buildings help it stand out from the crowd of similar towns in the area.

While the Teke peninsula has probably been occupied since around the Stone Age, Kas (pronounced cash) was originally established over Antiphellos, an ancient city that was also known as Habessus. Founded by the Lycians, the town's importance was confirmed by the fact that one of the richest Lycian necropolises was located in Kas.

The town was a tiny settlement area during the 4th century BC, and grew in size during the Hellenistic period, peaking in importance during both the Roman and Byzantine periods. Kas was then attacked by the Arabs, and named Andifli when it became part of the territory of Anatolian Seljuks. After the demise of the Seljuks, it came under Ottoman rule.

Kas suffered in 1923 when the exchange of populations meant that the majority of residents left to return to Greece, however it now thrives as a tourist town.

The main draw to Kas is the incredible diving spots which lures scuba divers from around the world. While the marine life doesn't quite measure up to the Red Sea, the visibility is still excellent and there are plenty of dive sites, including reefs, ship wrecks, and even plane wrecks. There are several dive centres to choose from, and they typically depart twice a day. Snorkelling is also popular here for those who aren't certified or don't want to take the time to learn to dive.

Kaputas Beach

The Çukurbağ Peninsula extends west of the old town, and you'll find an ancient theatre here which has been incredibly well-preserved. The Greek island of Meis is just offshore, and can be easily visited during a day trip.

If you'll be visiting on a Friday, be sure to visit the Friday Market, where you can try real Turkish delight, buy handmade trinkets, and shop for cheap clothes. If it's relaxation you are after, then the stunning Kaputas Beach is the place to go.

#19 Kalkan

© Flickr / Harry Luff

Kalkan is a harbor-side town built on hills, looking down on a picturesque bay. While the town can certainly be described as "enchanting", it's not the place to go if you're watching your budget. However an absence of mass tourism has meant that Kalkan remains unspoiled and charming, with crystal-clear sea, lush nature, ancient history, and warm hospitality.

The town is mainly devoted to high-end tourism, and with an average of 300 sunny days a year it's easy to see why. The white-washed houses, brightly colored bougainvillea plants, and many beautiful beaches make it the perfect place for a vacation.

Kalkan was both important and significant during the 19th century due to its strategic location. The coast was also famous for piracy, and the bay provided a convenient hiding place for the many pirates who would accost the merchant ships as they sailed by,

The Turkish and Greeks first settled in Kalkan during the Ottoman rule almost 200 years ago, and the town was a hub of trading, dealing in olive oil, wood, flour, grain, cotton, silk, wine, and many other goods.

Rapid development saw that Kalkan was well-populated by the early 20th century. However after WW1, and during the Turkish War of Independence, the Greeks migrated from the town.

Trading continued until the 1950's when improvements to infrastructure negated the need for sea trade. This meant that a large chunk of the population of Kalkan moved to larger cities to find work, however tourists soon began trickling, and then flooding into the town.

While it's unlikely you'll find any large clubs in Kalkan, there are numerous bars with live music, and restaurants with delicious Turkish and International options.

Kalkan is renowned for its water sports and scuba diving, and you can easily find lessons for scuba diving and water skiing, or hire canoes, speed boats and jet ski's.

Take the daily boat trip to the ancient castle of Simena and the sunken city of Kekova to see some interesting ruins. Sea tours also run to the ruins of Xanthos, which is a UNESCO World Heritage site. For those who simply want to lie on the beach, Patara is the place to go.

© Wikimedia / IzmirEkmek

Xanthos Ruins

Paragliding is also popular here, and at times you'll see up to 20 paragliders in the sky. The adventurers jump off Mount Babadag (you'll be attached to a pro) which is approximately 2000 metres high, or you can head to nearby Kas where the mountain is just 1000 metres high.

#20 Trabzon

© Wikimedia / İhsan Deniz Kılıçoğlu

Trabzon is located in the Eastern Black Sea region of Turkey, and is one of the major cities in the country. The city has an international airport, major roads connecting it to other cities, and a large harbor - in fact it's the busiest port in the Black Sea.

The city has a sophisticated, cosmopolitan atmosphere with a laid-back, seaside-town way of life. Trabzon is an enticing mix of old and new, with the modern world shining through in the busy main square of Ataturk Alani, and the elegant, medieval church/mosque of Aya Sofya.

At the end of the 4th century the Roman Empire was split in half, and Trabzon remained part of the Eastern Roman Empire, which later became the Byzantine Empire. The Byzantines considered Trabzon to be especially important for military purposes. During the 6th century when Emperor Justinian reigned, the city walls were enlarged and thoroughly repaired, huts were built for defence, and Christianity was established in order to create obedience.

In the 14th century Trabzon became the centre for Asia-Europe trade, however pirates were constantly raiding the coasts and attacking the city. Alexius Commenos constructed huge walls against the sea in order to protect the town, however Tamerlane invaded Trabzon at the beginning of the 15th century.

Over the next few centuries there were constant struggles over the throne, and the city passed hands continually. In 1912 the Italians took advantage of the instability in the region, and occupied the city which was owned by the Ottomans.

The Ottoman Government was continually changing hands, and finally in WW1 the Istanbul Government sided with Germany. Trabzon was bombed by 23 Russian warships, and was finally saved from the invasion in 1918, joining the Russian Empire. Following the Turkish War of Independence in 1920 Trabzon again became a part of Turkey.

The main attraction in Trabzon is the Aya Sofya Museum/church. It's thought that the church was originally built after Emperor Alexius Commenus arrived in Trabzon, and then converted into a mosque during the Ottoman period. Now it's a museum allowing visitors to see both Christian and Islamic ornaments.

Sümela Monastery

Trabzon has a fun nightlife, and the heart of it is set around the port, which is bursting with restaurants, bars, and cafes. The Bazaar district sells plenty of traditional hand-made items like scarves and bracelets, and the Forum Trabzon shopping centre is the best place to go for retail shopping.

Sitting 1200 metres above sea level the incredible Sumela Monastery is just 50km from Trabzon. The building was founded by two Greek monks in 386 AD, although it fell into ruin several times, it reached its present form in the 13th century. The whole building is full of wall paining and frescoes, and a large part of it was made out of the rock it is nestled into.

Map of the 20 Places to Visit in Turkey

#1 Istanbul

#2 Cappadocia

#3 Ephesus

#4 Marmaris

#5 Antalya

#6 Oludeniz

#7 Bodrum

#8 Side

#9 Ankara

#10 Pamukkale

#11 Kusadasi

#12 Konya

#13 Izmir

#14 Fethiye

#15 Alanya

#16 Dalyan

#17 Mardin

#18 Kas

#19 Kalkan

#20 Trabzon

A Note to the Reader

Dear Reader

Thank you for your purchase of this Atsons Travel guide, we hope you have enjoyed reading it!

Please feel free to post an informative, unbiased review on Amazon so that others may benefit from your experience. A Review would be greatly appreciated as it helps us spread the word of our books and attract more fantastic customers such as yourselves.

Also your feedback is invaluable to us, as we work hard to serve you and continually improve our customers' experience.

Sincerely

Atsons Travel Guides

Printed in Great Britain
by Amazon

87393553R00027